Oliver Twist

Charles Dickens

About this Book

For the Student

Listen to all of the story and do some activities on your Audio CD

Talk about the story

tune• When you see the orange dot you can check the word in the glossary

K Prepare for Cambridge English: Key (KET) for Schools

For the Teacher

e•ZONE THE EDUCATIONAL PLATFORM A state-of-the-art interactive learning environment with 1000s of free online self-correcting activities for your chosen readers.

Go to our Readers Resource site for information on using readers and downloadable Resource Sheets, photocopiable Worksheets and Answer Keys. Plus free sample tracks from the story.

www.helblingreaders.com

For lots of great ideas on using Graded Readers consult Reading Matters, the Teacher's Guide to using Helbling Readers.

Level 3 Structures

Present continuous for future	Cardinal / ordinal numbers
Present perfect	*One / ones*
Present perfect versus past simple	Reflexive pronouns
Should / shouldn't (advice and obligation)	Indefinite pronouns
Must / should	
Need to / have to	*Too* plus adjective
Will	*Not* plus adjective plus *enough*
	Relative pronouns *who, which* and *that*
Ever / never	Prepositions of time, place and movement
Would like	
So do I / neither do I	
Question tags	

Structures from lower levels are also included

Contents

HELBLING DIGITAL

INTERACTIVE ONLINE TEACHING AND LEARNING MATERIALS

e·zone
THE EDUCATIONAL PLATFORM

HELBLING e-zone is an inspiring new state-of-the-art, easy-to-use interactive learning environment.

The online self-correcting activities include:

- reading comprehension;
- listening comprehension;
- vocabulary;
- grammar;
- exam preparation.

TEACHERS register free of charge to set up classes and assign individual and class homework sets. Results are provided automatically once the deadline has been reached and detailed reports on performance are available at a click.

STUDENTS test their language skills in a stimulating interactive environment. All activities can be attempted as many times as necessary and full results and feedback are given as soon as the deadline has been reached. Single student access is also available.

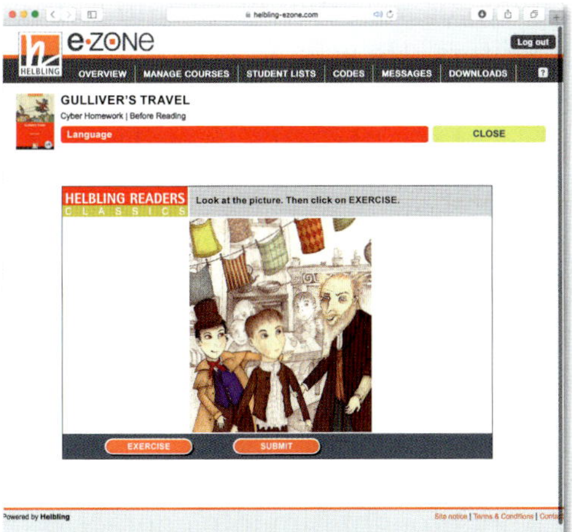

1000s of free online interactive activities now available for HELBLING READERS and your other favourite Helbling Languages publications.

ONLINE ACTIVITIES

helbling-ezone.com

blog.helblingreaders.com

Love reading and readers and can't wait to get your class interested? Have a class library and reading programme but not sure how to take it a step further? The Helbling Readers BLOG is the place for you.

The **Helbling Readers BLOG** will provide you with ideas on setting up and running a Book Club and tips on reading lessons **every week**.

- Book Club
- Worksheets
- Lesson Plans

Subscribe to our **BLOG** and you will never miss out on our updates.

ABOUT THE AUTHOR

Charles Dickens was one of Britain's most popular writers. He was born in Portsea, in the south of England, in 1812, but Dickens spent most of his life in London. He had a difficult childhood. He grew up in a family that never had enough money. His father could not earn enough money to support his ten children and he lived in a debtors' prison•. At the early age of 12, Dickens had to start working in a factory.

As a young man Dickens found work first in an office and then as a journalist. His newspaper work brought him into contact with many different people. He enjoyed writing detailed descriptions of the people he met, their clothing, their habits, and their way of talking. He witnessed• the hardship• and tragedy of life, as well as its humorous• side.

Soon Dickens started writing stories that he published in monthly instalments•. His first novel *The Pickwick Papers* had a small following• at first, but then it started selling 40,000 copies per instalment. After this he wrote many more novels and travelled throughout Britain and America doing dramatic readings of his most loved books. Among the most famous were *David Copperfield*, *Great Expectations*, *Bleak House*, *A Christmas Carol*, *A Tale of Two Cities,* and *Oliver Twist*. Dickens' work presented to readers a new type of novel illustrating, through fiction, the most important social problems of the period. Charles Dickens died in 1870.

Glossary

- **debtors' prison:** prison for people who owed money/were in debt
- **following:** people who read it
- **hardship:** difficult side (of life)
- **humorous:** funny
- **instalments:** parts
- **witnessed:** saw

ABOUT THE BOOK

Oliver Twist (written between 1837 and 38) brings to life the character of a poor lonely orphan. Oliver suffers all types of problems, evil influences and cruel treatment from adults but he remains innocent and pure at heart.

Like Oliver, Dickens himself experienced the horrors of the workhouse•, where people who were very poor were sent to work. Like Oliver, too, Dickens had to go to work at a very young age. Dickens worked in a factory while Oliver becomes an apprentice•.

Through *Oliver Twist*, Dickens illustrates the social injustices• of his time. Extreme poverty• led to crime•, but also to people being severely punished for minor• crimes.

The London of Dickens is a dark and evil place. Dickens shows us the squalor• of the streets and the buildings that are inhabited by Fagin and his boys. This contrasts with the calm, beautiful countryside where Mrs Maylie and Rose live in peace and comfort. There are also contrasts between the characters who want to help Oliver and protect him, and those characters who want to exploit• Oliver and each other.

Oliver is innocent and trusting, but throughout the novel he falls into the hands of dishonest people. They sell him, they rob him, they kidnap him, they make him ill, but Dickens shows that in the end good can be stronger than evil.

- **apprentice:** person who is learning a job
- **crime:** illegal actions
- **exploit:** use
- **injustices:** things that are not fair
- **minor:** not important
- **poverty:** when you are poor
- **squalor:** dirty, bad conditions
- **workhouse:** place where poor people worked in exchange for food and a place to sleep

BEFORE READING

1 Look at the pictures in the book and read the descriptions. Which one describes Oliver Twist? Tick (✓).

a) ☐ He is eleven years old but is small and fat for his age. He has short dark hair and brown eyes.

b) ☐ She has long dark brown hair and her eyes are blue. She is tall and thin but we do not know how old she is.

c) ☒ He has short brown hair and blue eyes. He's thin and he isn't very tall. He's about nine years old.

2 Read these sentences about Oliver and choose a word from the box to describe him.

clever	tired	hungry	innocent

a) Every day in the workhouse, Oliver only got thin soup to eat. Oliver was very ...hungry... .

b) Oliver walked and walked for twenty miles to get to London. Oliver was ...tired... .

c) Oliver quickly learned everything that Fagin taught him. Oliver was ...clever... .

d) Oliver didn't rob anyone, but the police officer thought he was a thief. Oliver was ...innocent... .

3 What do you think Oliver is doing in this picture? Tick (✓).

a) ☒ Asking for more food.

b) ☐ Walking to London.

c) ☐ Talking to a police officer.

4 **Listen and match the characters to the descriptions.**

a) ☐

Mr Brownlow

b) ☐

Fagin

c) ☐

Nancy

d) ☐

Oliver

5 **Listen to these extracts from the story. Do the characters in the pictures like or dislike Oliver? Tick (✓).**

A **Mr Bumble**

Like ☐ Dislike ☐

B **Mrs Bedwin**

Like ☐ Dislike ☐

C **Monks**

Like ☐ Dislike ☐

D **Sikes**

Like ☐ Dislike ☐

BEFORE READING

1 Look at the pictures of these places from *Oliver Twist*. Then match them with the descriptions below.

1 orphanage

2 country house

3 workhouse

4 bookstall

5 police station

6 cottage

a) The police investigate crimes in this building.
b) People who enjoy reading can choose and buy books here.
c) Children who have no mother or father live in this place.
d) Rich people can live and enjoy the beauty of the countryside here.
e) This is a small house in the country, close to a village.
f) This is a large building where very poor people live and work.

2 Who says the following? Match the word to the sentence.

orphan servant thief

a) I steal things from other people. ...thief...
b) I have no mother or father. ...orphan...
c) I work in someone's house, cooking and cleaning. ...servant...

3 Here are some words from the story. Match them with the pictures.

a) wedding ring
b) handkerchief
c) pocket
d) soup
e) cloak
f) portrait
g) knife
h) watch

1 

2 

3 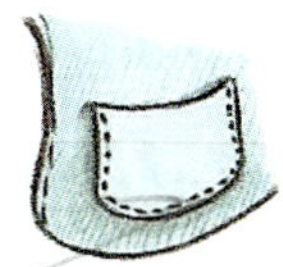

4 

5 

6 

7 

8 

4 Use the words from Exercise 3 to complete these sentences.

a) Oliver's mother was not wearing a .... so probably she was not married.

b) Nancy wore a .... to keep her warm when she went outside.

c) There was a .... of a beautiful lady on the wall of Oliver's room.

d) The children at the workhouse ate .... every day.

e) In Fagin's room there was a .... for cutting bread.

f) Fagin put a .... and a .... in the .... of his jacket and the boys tried to steal them from him.

1 OLIVER ENTERS THE WORLD

4 Oliver Twist was born in a workhouse•. When Oliver was born, there was no one to look after him except for an old nurse and a doctor. They didn't care about him.

Oliver's mother arrived at the workhouse the night before she gave birth to her son. She asked to see her baby and then died. No one knew where she came from or who she was. But the doctor noticed• that she had no wedding ring on her finger.

When the doctor left and the old nurse dressed him, Oliver cried loudly. He was an orphan and he was all alone. There was no one to look after baby Oliver at the workhouse so he was sent to an orphanage•. Life was hard here, with little food or love.

By the age of nine, Oliver was a small pale thin child, but he had a strong spirit. The housekeeper• of the orphanage was cruel• and hard. She often beat• Oliver and locked him up. This was usually for saying he was hungry.

One day the housekeeper was surprised by a visit from Mr Bumble, the head of the workhouse.

'Oliver Twist is nine years old now. He's too old to stay here at the orphanage with you,' Mr Bumble said. 'So, we have decided to move him to the workhouse. I have come here myself to collect him and take him there.'

Glossary

- **beat:** hit
- **cruel:** unkind
- **housekeeper:** person employed to look after a house
- **noticed:** saw
- **orphanage:** home for children with no mother or father
- **workhouse:** place where poor people worked in exchange for food and a place to sleep

As soon as they arrived at the workhouse, Mr Bumble took Oliver to meet the Board•. The Board consisted of nine or ten fat gentlemen sitting around a table.

'Boy,' said one of the fat gentlemen to Oliver, 'you are an orphan and you must be grateful• for the charity• of the town. Pray hard for the people who feed• you. You are here to learn a trade•, and you will begin your work tomorrow morning. Goodnight.'

And poor little Oliver was sent to sleep on a hard cold bed in a room full of other boys, to be ready for work the next morning.

There was even less food at the workhouse than at the orphanage. The boys got three meals of thin soup a day, with an onion in it twice a week, and half a piece of bread on Sundays. The boys got hungrier and hungrier until one day they decided to do something. One boy had to ask for more food at supper that evening. They drew lots•: Oliver Twist was that boy.

DRAWING LOTS

Work in groups of six.
Put together a collection of 'lots.' They can be pencils with one shorter than all the others or pieces of paper, one marked with a sign.
Then draw lots.
Decide on a question to ask the teacher. The student with the shortest pencil or with the paper with a mark must ask the teacher the question.

Glossary

- **Board:** group of people who manage an institution
- **charity:** help given to poor people
- **drew lots:** played a game of chance to choose someone
- **feed:** give someone food
- **grateful:** thankful
- **trade:** job

The evening arrived and the boys took their places in the dining hall. The master of the workhouse stood by the cooking pot and served out the soup. Soon there was no more soup and the boys were desperate with hunger.

Oliver rose from the table and walked up to the master. He held up his bowl and said, 'Please, sir, I want some more.'

The master turned very pale when he heard Oliver's request. The boys froze with fear as they waited for his answer.

'What?' said the master.

'Please, sir,' repeated Oliver. 'I want some more.'

The master hit Oliver on the head with his serving spoon, and called Mr Bumble.

The Board was in a meeting when Mr Bumble rushed in and interrupted them.

'Excuse me, sir!' said Mr Bumble to the gentleman in the high chair. 'Oliver Twist has asked for more!'

'For more?' said the gentleman. 'The boy is an ungrateful criminal and he must leave the workhouse!'

They locked Oliver up. For a whole week, he was locked in a dark, solitary room, crying all day and having nightmares all night.

HUNGER

When you are hungry how do you feel?
Tell a friend.

Glossary

- **bowl:** 
- **criminal:** person who has committed crimes
- **nightmares:** bad dreams
- **rose:** stood up
- **rushed in:** entered in a great hurry

2 OLIVER GETS A JOB

Mr Bumble bumped into• Mr Sowerberry, the undertaker•, who was a frequent visitor to the workhouse.

'Do you know anyone who wants a boy as an apprentice•?' asked Mr Bumble. 'We are offering five pounds to anyone who will take Oliver Twist.'

'Five pounds!' said the undertaker. 'I think I'll take the boy myself.'

When the undertaker's wife saw Oliver, she said, 'Dear me! He's very small.' She gave him a few pieces of old meat and then she led him upstairs and showed him his bed on the floor of the shop. Alone and surrounded by coffins•, Oliver felt very sad that night.

Early next morning, a voice woke Oliver.

'Open the door,' cried the voice.

'Yes, sir,' replied Oliver. 'Do you want a coffin, sir?'

'Don't you know who I am?' said the voice. 'I'm Mr Noah Claypole, and you work for me now.'

Noah was only a poor boy who worked for Mr Sowerberry. But he was very happy to have someone new and small like Oliver to give orders to.

Then, one evening, Mr Sowerberry had an idea.

'Oliver Twist is a very good-looking boy,' he said to his wife. 'And he always looks very sad. He will come with me to the next funeral•.'

Glossary

- **apprentice:** person learning a job
- **bumped into:** met by chance
- **coffins:** large boxes for bodies of dead people
- **funeral:** church service for dead people
- **mournful:** very sad
- **undertaker:** person who buries dead people

Oliver followed instructions and went with Mr Sowerberry to the next funeral. His job was to stand there and look sad.

'Well, Oliver,' said Mr Sowerberry as they walked home, 'how do you like it?'

'Not very much, sir.'

So Oliver became assistant to the undertaker and, dressed all in black, he led many mournful• processions.

Noah was jealous of Oliver's new job and he became meaner than before. Mrs Sowerberry disliked Oliver because Mr Sowerberry liked him.

One evening, Oliver and Noah were alone together in the kitchen. Noah started to talk badly about Oliver's mother and call her names. Oliver grew red with anger and hit Noah hard.

'Help! He'll kill me! Help!' shouted Noah.

That night they locked Oliver in the cellar. The next morning Mrs Sowerberry sent Noah to get Mr Bumble from the workhouse. Oliver was still in the cellar, kicking at the door when he arrived.

'He must be mad, Mr Bumble,' said Mrs Sowerberry. 'Why does he act like this?'

'It's your fault, madam,' said Mr Bumble. 'You gave him too much to eat. And remember. He comes from a bad family. He's just like his mother.'

When Oliver heard Mr Bumble mention his mother, he started kicking again. Poor Oliver. They beat him and locked him up again, then they sent him to sleep with the coffins. In the darkness, Oliver sat on the floor and wept bitterly.

By the light of a candle, Oliver tied some clothes into a large handkerchief and waited for the morning. As soon as the first rays of light came through the window, he got up, unlocked the door and escaped into the street.

ESCAPE

Where do you think Oliver will go?

Glossary

- **bitterly:** in an unhappy way
- **cellar:** dark room at the bottom of a house
- **handkerchief:** 
- **it's your fault:** you are responsible
- **rays:** light from the sun

3 OLIVER MAKES NEW FRIENDS

6 Oliver set off• in the direction of London. 'No one will find me in London,' he thought. He walked and he walked for twenty miles, then he lay down in a field and fell asleep. He walked for seven more days, begging• for food and water. Then on the seventh day he walked slowly into a small town and sat down to rest. His feet were bleeding• and he was covered in dirt•. A boy saw him and came to talk to him.

'Hello, where have you been?' asked the boy.

The boy was about the same age as Oliver, but he was a strange-looking boy. He had a large hat and he wore a man's coat, which came nearly to his feet. He was just a dirty little boy but he acted and talked like an adult.

'I've walked for seven days,' said Oliver. 'I'm very tired and hungry.'

'Well,' said the boy, 'come with me and I'll get you something to eat.'

The boy bought Oliver some food. Then, as Oliver ate hungrily, they talked.

'Are you going to London?' the boy asked.

'Yes,' Oliver replied.

'Have you got anywhere to stay?'

'No.'

'I know an old gentleman who lives in London,' said the boy. 'He'll give you a place to stay for nothing.'

Oliver was thankful for this offer. His new friend was Jack Dawkins, but Jack's friends called him the Dodger•.

- **begging:** asking
- **bleeding:** with blood coming out
- **dirt:** earth or soil from the ground
- **set off:** started walking
- **the Dodger:** someone who is good at robbing people without being seen

Late that night they reached• London. The Dodger led Oliver to a narrow smelly street, and into a house. They climbed the stairs and went into a room at the top.

Oliver looked around. They were in a large room. The walls and ceiling were black with age and dirt. A man was cooking some food in a frying pan over a fire. The man had an ugly face and dirty red hair. There were beds on the floor. Four or five boys, about the same age as the Dodger, sat around a table.

'Fagin,' said the Dodger, 'this is my friend Oliver Twist.'

The man grinned•, then he shook Oliver's hand and said, 'We are very glad to meet you, Oliver.'

Oliver noticed some handkerchiefs hanging on a line•.

'Those handkerchiefs are going to be washed, Oliver,' said Fagin and he laughed. After this they all had supper. Oliver ate a lot and then he drank a nightcap• that Fagin prepared specially for him. After this he fell into a deep sleep.

FAGIN

Look at Fagin. Describe him.

Do you think Oliver can trust him? Why?/Why not?

Discuss in small groups.

Glossary

- **grinned:** smiled
- **line:** (see illustration page 22)
- **nightcap:** drink that you have at bedtime to help you sleep
- **reached:** arrived at

4 OLIVER LEARNS SOME SKILLS

7 The next morning when Oliver woke up, Fagin was making coffee and whistling• softly to himself. The boys were gone and Oliver was curious so he pretended to be still asleep. He watched as Fagin took a small box from a hole in the floor. He put it onto the table and he took from it rings, bracelets, necklaces, and a magnificent gold watch. Fagin looked up and saw that Oliver was watching. He closed the lid• of the box with a loud crash.

'Why are you watching me?' he said, grabbing• a bread knife and standing up.

'I'm very sorry, sir,' said Oliver, terrified. 'I woke up and saw you.'

Fagin put down the knife.

'Did you see any of the pretty things in the box?'

'Yes, sir,' said Oliver.

'Those things are mine, Oliver. I am saving them for when I am old.'

Fagin sent Oliver to wash his face. When Oliver came back, Fagin's box was gone.

Shortly after, the Dodger returned with his friend Charley Bates.

'Have you been at work this morning, my boys?' Fagin asked the Dodger and Charley. 'What have you got?'

'A couple of wallets•,' said the Dodger, handing them to Fagin.

'Not as heavy as I expected,' said Fagin, looking inside them, 'but very well made. What about you, Charley?' said Fagin.

Charley showed him four handkerchiefs.

'Very good,' said Fagin. 'Now we'll teach Oliver.'

'Yes, please, sir,' said Oliver.

The boys started laughing.

Glossary

- **grabbing:** taking quickly and with force
- **lid:** cover for a container
- **wallets:** small leather cases containing money
- **whistling:** musical sound made with your lips

After breakfast, Fagin and the two boys played a very curious game. Fagin put a silver box in one pocket of his trousers and a wallet in the other, and a watch in his jacket pocket. He walked around the room, then stopped and pretended to look into shop windows. The two boys followed him. At last the Dodger stood on Fagin's foot and at the same time Charley fell against him. In that moment they took from him, with extraordinary speed, the silver box, wallet, watch and handkerchief.

Then, later on, the Dodger and Charley went out to find more work.

'There, my dear,' said Fagin to Oliver, 'you should follow their example. Now tell me, is my handkerchief hanging out of my pocket?'

'Yes, sir.'

'See if you can take it out, without my feeling it.'

Oliver copied the Dodger's actions and pulled out the handkerchief.

'Here it is, sir,' said Oliver.

'Clever boy,' said Fagin, patting Oliver on the head. 'Here's a coin for you.'

GAME

What 'game' are they playing?

- **coin:** 
- **game:** activity played for fun by a group of people
- **patting:** touching gently with your hand
- **speed:** when you are fast

OKS
J B
J B

A few days later, Fagin sent Oliver out to work with the Dodger and Charley.

They walked until they came to a small square. Then the Dodger pointed to an elderly man who was reading books at a bookstall•.

'He'll do•,' said Charley.

The two boys walked across the road, and stood behind the old gentleman. Oliver stood and watched. The old gentleman looked very respectable. He stood there reading. He was very relaxed. But then Oliver was horrified to see the Dodger carefully put his hand into the old gentleman's pocket and take out a handkerchief. Oliver saw him give the handkerchief to Charley, and he saw them both run away around the corner at full speed.

In an instant, the mystery of the handkerchiefs, and the watches, and Fagin, was clear in Oliver's mind.

Oliver turned and started running as fast as he could. Meanwhile, the old gentleman put his hand in his pocket and found his handkerchief was missing. He saw Oliver running away and he thought that Oliver was the thief. The old gentleman shouted, 'Stop thief!' and ran after him.

The Dodger and Charley hid in a doorway• around the corner. When they saw Oliver running, they also ran after him and shouted, 'Stop thief!'

In this way everyone believed that Oliver was the thief. Everyone in the neighbourhood• ran after Oliver. There was a mad chase• through the streets. Oliver tried to run faster, but he tripped•. He fell onto the pavement• and cut his face.

Glossary

- **bookstall:** type of bookshop
- **chase:** when you run to catch someone
- **doorway:** entrance
- **he'll do:** we'll choose him
- **neighbourhood:** local area
- **pavement:** part of a street where people walk
- **tripped:** fell over

A police officer came through the crowd, and seized Oliver by the collar. 'Get up,' he said.

'It wasn't me, sir. It was the other two boys,' said Oliver. 'They are here somewhere.'

'Oh no, they aren't,' said the police officer. He dragged Oliver away with him to the police station and locked him in a cell.

The old gentleman followed Oliver to the police station and asked to speak to the officer in charge.

'Who are you?' said the police officer.

'My name is Brownlow,' said the gentleman. 'I was standing at the bookstall, reading a book and two boys robbed me. The boy you have is innocent,' he said.

'Bring the boy here,' said the police officer.

Oliver was very pale. He was so afraid that he couldn't speak.

'Did this boy rob you?' the officer asked Mr Brownlow.

'No, he did not,' said Mr Brownlow.

'In that case,' said the officer, 'I am discharging him.'

Little Oliver Twist lay shaking on the ground. His face was completely white. Mr Brownlow put him into a carriage.

'Quickly,' he said to the driver. 'There is no time to lose.'

MR BROWNLOW

What type of person is Mr Brownlow?
Discuss in small groups.

Glossary

- **carriage:** vehicle pulled by horses
- **cell:** room inside a prison
- **discharging:** releasing
- **dragged:** pulled
- **officer in charge:** policeman in command
- **robbed me:** took things from me

5 THE PORTRAIT

8

'Where am I?' said Oliver, lifting his head from his pillow.

Mrs Bedwin, Mr Brownlow's housekeeper, was sitting by Oliver's bed. 'Hush•, my dear,' she said, 'try to rest.' With these words, she smoothed• Oliver's hair back from his forehead.

'Imagine what your mother is thinking right now!' said Mrs Bedwin.

'Perhaps she can see me,' whispered Oliver. 'I feel she is here with me.'

'That was the fever•, my dear,' said Mrs Bedwin.

'I suppose it was,' said Oliver. 'The angels are too happy in heaven to come to the bedside of a poor boy.'

After saying these words, Oliver fell into a deep sleep.

Three days passed. Oliver was still too weak to walk, but he was able to sit in an armchair.

'You're very kind to me, ma'am•,' said Oliver.

'Just eat your soup,' said Mrs Bedwin.

On the wall opposite there was a portrait of a young woman. Oliver stared• at it. 'What a beautiful face that lady has!' he said. 'But her eyes look so sad. She looks as if she is alive, and wants to speak to me.'

There was a soft knock• at the door, and Mr Brownlow came in.

'Poor boy,' said Mr Brownlow. 'How do you feel?'

'Very happy, sir,' said Oliver, 'and very grateful for your kindness to me.'

- **fever:** high body temperature
- **hush:** don't say anything
- **knock:** bang
- **ma'am:** madam
- **smoothed:** moved gently
- **stared:** looked for a long time

At that moment, Mr Brownlow saw the similarity between Oliver's features and another familiar face.

'Mrs Bedwin,' he said, 'look at this!' He pointed to the portrait on the wall and then to Oliver's face. Oliver was the living copy of the portrait. The eyes, the head, the mouth... every feature was the same.

6 MISSING PERSON

9 'What's happened to Oliver?' said Fagin. He grabbed the Dodger by the collar.

'Let me go,' said the Dodger. 'The police have got him.'

'What's going on•?' growled• a deep voice. The man who spoke was Bill Sikes, a tall strong man of about thirty-five.

'Bill,' said Fagin, 'we must find our new boy Oliver before he talks to the police. We don't want any trouble.'

There was a noise at the door and a young woman arrived.

'Nancy, my dear,' said Fagin. 'You can help us find young Oliver.'

'Find him yourself,' said Nancy.

'Be kind,' said Fagin. 'We have to find out where he is.'

'Do we have to kidnap• him?' said the Dodger.

'Find him first,' said Fagin. 'I'll know what to do next.'

OLIVER

How many people are looking for Oliver? Underline their names in the text.
Why do they want to find Oliver?

Glossary

- **going on:** happening
- **growled:** made a noise like an angry dog
- **kidnap:** catch like a prisoner

Oliver hurried towards the bookshop, thinking how happy and contented he felt. Suddenly a young woman grabbed him and threw her arms tightly around his neck. It was Nancy.

'Oh, my dear brother!' she shouted loudly for everyone in the street to hear.

'Let go of me!' cried Oliver, struggling•. 'Who are you?'

'Oh! Oliver! You naughty boy. Come home, dear, come home,' cried Nancy. 'Thank goodness, I've found you!' She burst into tears.

'What's this?' said a big man, who came out of a shop. It was Bill Sikes. 'Oliver,' he said, 'come home to your poor mother right now!'

'Help! Help!' cried Oliver, struggling in Sikes' powerful grip•. But no one heard him.

'Oh, Fagin, look who's coming,' shouted Charley Bates, as Sikes, Nancy and Oliver came up the broken stairs.

'I'm delighted to see you looking so well, Oliver,' said Fagin.

'Look at his clothes, Fagin!' Charley walked all around Oliver, viewing him. The Dodger examined his pockets and found the five pound note.

'You can keep the books, Fagin,' said Sikes. 'I'll take the money.'

'Please send the books and money back to Mr Brownlow,' begged Oliver.

'Oh dear, Oliver,' laughed Fagin. 'Now Mr Brownlow thinks you're a thief.'

Oliver turned and ran towards the door, but the two boys ran after him and brought him back. Fagin hit Oliver with a stick. Nancy tried to stop him but Sikes pushed her away.

'Charley,' Fagin shouted, 'take Oliver's new clothes and show him to "bed"•.'

Glossary

- **grip:** holding tightly with his hand
- **show him to 'bed':** take him to the place where he will sleep
- **struggling:** (here) fighting to escape

7 THE TRUTH ABOUT OLIVER

Mr Bumble was in London on business. After dinner he sat by the fire and read the newspaper. That's when he saw the following advertisement:

> **TWENTY POUNDS REWARD**
>
> A young boy named **Oliver Twist** went missing from his home last Thursday evening. There is a reward for anyone who knows where he is.

Underneath was the name and address of Mr Brownlow. Mr Bumble went there immediately.

'So, Mr Bumble, you are here because you saw the advertisement,' said Mr Brownlow. 'Do you know where this poor boy Oliver is now?'

Mr Bumble knew very little, but he explained that Oliver was an orphan.

'He comes from a bad family, and when I knew him in the workhouse, he was a terrible, ungrateful and violent child.'

'I'm afraid you must be right,' said Mr Brownlow sadly. 'Thank you for your help, Mr Bumble.'

Mr Bumble took his reward money and left.

'It can't be true,' said Mrs Bedwin. 'Oliver's a good boy.'

'Silence,' said Mr Brownlow. 'I never want to hear that boy's name again.'

Glossary

- **advertisement:** notice with information
- **reward:** (here) money given in return for information
- **underneath:** under
- **went missing:** disappeared

8 THE ROBBERY

11

For many days Oliver stayed locked up in Fagin's house. There were spiders' webs• and mice and the shutters• of the windows were always closed. Oliver sat waiting for the boys to come back.

Every day Oliver and the other boys played the stealing game with Fagin. Sometimes the old man told them stories of when he was young and all the things he stole. In this way Fagin prepared Oliver's mind to prefer the company of criminals.

Soon the time came when Oliver had to work for his bread•. Sikes was planning a big robbery.

'You must find us a boy, and he mustn't be too big,' Sikes told Fagin.

'Oliver's the boy for you, Bill,' said Fagin. 'I've trained him well these last few weeks. He will do everything you want, Bill, my dear. He's one of us, now.'

That evening Nancy came to collect Oliver. Fagin gave him some advice before he left.

'Be careful, Oliver,' he said. 'Bill Sikes is a rough• man. Whatever happens, say nothing, and always do what he tells you.'

Oliver's heart trembled. He didn't like Bill Sikes.

Nancy took Oliver to Sikes' house.

'Come here, Oliver,' Sikes said when he saw him. 'And listen to the rules.'

Oliver came forward.

'Don't speak a word when you're with me, Oliver, or I will use this gun• on you.'

- **bread:** (here) food and a place to live
- **gun:** 
- **rough:** (here) not gentle
- **shutters:** pieces of wood covering the windows
- **spiders' webs:** 

The wind blew and it rained hard when they started their journey. Sikes dragged Oliver along with him. They walked a long way into the countryside. Oliver wondered where Sikes was taking him. They arrived at a dark house. Inside, another man was waiting for them. He was Toby Crackit, Sikes' business partner. Crackit looked surprised when he saw Oliver.

'He's one of Fagin's boys,' said Sikes. 'He's working with us tonight. We'll eat something now and rest before we go out.'

Later the two men left the dark house with Oliver between them. Outside it was dark and freezing cold. The church bell struck two. They came to a big grand house surrounded by a wall. They all climbed the wall.

Suddenly Oliver realised that they were going to steal something from the house. He put his hands together, and fell to his knees.

'Please let me go!' he cried, in terror. 'Do not make me steal.'

'Get up!' said Sikes, trembling with anger. 'Get up and be quiet or I'll shoot you.'

They came to a small window and Crackit opened it. It was large enough for a small boy to enter.

'Now listen,' Sikes whispered to Oliver, 'I'm going to put you through the window. When you are inside, go to the main door. Open it, and let us in.'

Sikes put Oliver through the window with his feet first.

'Remember! One mistake and I'll shoot you dead,' said Sikes.

Oliver wanted to warn the family in the house. He wasn't scared of Sikes. He took a chance and ran towards the stairs, not the main door.

'Come back!' shouted Sikes. 'Come back!'

Oliver heard Sikes shouting, then he saw a light. He saw two men at the top of the stairs. He heard a loud noise and felt a terrible pain. Confused, Oliver moved back to the small window. He heard Sikes call out, 'They've hit him. Quick! He's bleeding!'

Oliver's heart felt cold. The noises grew confused in the distance. Then he saw and heard no more.

9 OLD SALLY'S SECRET

12 'Who's that?' cried old Sally. She was weak and dying but she was able to lift up her head when Mrs Corney, the mistress• of the workhouse, entered.

'Come nearer!' said Sally. 'Let me whisper in your ear.' She held Mrs Corney by the arm.

'Listen to me,' said the dying woman. 'In this room, I once looked after a pretty young woman. She had a baby boy, and she died shortly after.'

Sally's face was flushed•.

'I robbed her,' she said. 'I stole the only thing she had, some gold jewellery. The boy grew to be so like his mother. I could never forget her when I saw his face. Poor girl! She was so young.'

Mrs Corney, leaned• close to Sally to hear her words.

'Before she died, the mother said she wanted me to help her child.'

'What was the boy's name?' asked Mrs Corney.

'They called him Oliver,' said Sally. 'The gold I stole was...'

'Yes, yes, what?' said Mrs Corney, trying to hear Sally's reply. Old Sally held Mrs Corney's arm with both hands, then fell back onto the bed. She was dead.

OLD SALLY

Who do you think old Sally is?
Go back to page 13 and find out.

Glossary

- **flushed:** red in the face
- **leaned:** moved close
- **mistress:** (here) woman in position of authority

10 A MEETING WITH MONKS

13 Toby Crackit came back to London to tell Fagin what happened.

'The robbery failed,' said Crackit. 'They chased us but we escaped across the fields.'

'What about Oliver?' said Fagin.

'They shot him with a gun. We left him lying in a ditch•. I don't know if he is alive or dead.'

'But that boy is worth hundreds of pounds to me,' said Fagin angrily. 'I mustn't lose him. Now go!'

Fagin unlocked the door and pushed Crackit out onto the street.

Then a man's voice whispered in Fagin's ear, 'Fagin!'

'Monks!' said Fagin. 'Follow me.' He took Monks to a room on the first floor and put a candle on the floor.

Monks and Fagin sat down opposite each other. They talked in whispers•. Then Monks raised his voice and said, 'The robbery was badly planned. Why didn't you keep him here and teach him to be a pickpocket•?'

WHISPERS

Get into groups of three.

Student One thinks of a secret and tells Student Two, talking only in whispers.

Can Student Three hear what you are saying?

Change roles.

- **ditch:** long hole by the side of a road
- **in whispers:** in very quiet voices
- **pickpocket:** person who steals things from people's pockets

'He was different from the other boys,' said Fagin. 'We tried to send him out with the Dodger and Charley Bates, but it didn't work. Do you want him to be a thief? If he is alive, I can teach him. But, if he is dead...'

'It's not my fault if he's dead!' said Monks. 'I had nothing to do with it. If they shot him dead, I was not the cause.' He stopped speaking and looked around. Then he said, 'What's that?'

'What!' said Fagin. 'Where?'

'Over there!' said Monks. 'I saw something. Was it a woman?'

The two men rushed from the room but there was no one outside. They listened, but the house was silent.

'It's your imagination,' said Fagin.

'Yes, you're right,' said Monks. 'Goodnight, Fagin. We will speak of the boy again, when we know if he is dead or alive.'

11 THE WOUNDED THIEF IS LOOKED AFTER

14 Oliver lay in the ditch where Sikes left him. After some time he woke up and saw that his left arm was covered in blood. Oliver got up. In front of him, he saw the house from the robbery and he walked slowly towards it. He knocked at the door, then fell down. A servant opened the door and recognised him immediately.

'Here he is!' the servant shouted. 'Here's one of the thieves, madam! Here's the thief we shot!'

A lady's voice from inside the house said, 'Well, bring him inside and then run to get Dr Losberne.'

The two ladies who lived in the house, Mrs Maylie and her niece Miss Rose, waited for news about the wounded thief from the doctor.

The door of the upstairs bedroom opened.

'You can come and see him now,' said Dr Losberne.

Dr Losberne pulled back the curtains of the bed. The ladies gasped•. They expected to see a rough thief. Instead they saw only a child in a deep sleep.

'Is it really possible that this delicate boy is a terrible thief?' asked Rose.

'It is possible. When he wakes up I will question him,' said Dr Losberne. 'Then we can decide what to do with him.'

Hour after hour passed, and Oliver slept. He didn't wake up until the evening. He told them his story but he often had to stop because he was so weak• and in pain. His story was sad and when Dr Losberne finished his questions, he made Oliver comfortable and let him fall asleep again.

Glossary

- **gasped:** made a sound of surprise
- **weak:** with no energy

Rose and Mrs Maylie looked after Oliver well, and slowly he began to get better. Dr Losberne visited often and they became good friends. Gradually Oliver grew strong and healthy. He started studying lessons and he played in the garden.

Then one evening Oliver fell asleep while he was reading his book and he had a bad dream. He woke up suddenly. There at the window, right in front of him, was Fagin. Their eyes met. There was another man beside him. In an instant, they disappeared. Oliver called loudly for help. Everyone searched for the men, but they could not find any footprints•.

'It was a dream, Oliver,' said Dr Losberne.

'No, sir, it wasn't,' said Oliver. He trembled as he remembered Fagin's face. 'I saw them both as clearly as I can see you now.'

Dr Losberne watched Oliver's face and believed him, but there was no sign of anyone. After a few days, everyone had forgotten the incident. Everyone except for Oliver.

FACES

Can you remember people's faces?
Who do you remember more, people you like or people you don't like?
Tell a friend.

Glossary

- **footprints:** marks of feet on the ground

12 MR BUMBLE AND THE STRANGER

Mr Bumble was now married to Mrs Corney, the mistress of the workhouse. They seemed to argue and fight all the time. But at least he was now the master of the workhouse and not just an official. One evening, after another argument with his wife, Mr Bumble walked down the road and stopped at a public house•. There was one other customer there, a tall, dark man who wore a long cloak•. He looked at Mr Bumble but said nothing. Mr Bumble drank in silence and read the newspaper. Every now and then he looked over at the stranger, and each time he looked, the stranger was looking at him, too.

After a while the stranger said, 'I have seen you before. You're an official at the workhouse, aren't you?'

'I was,' said Mr Bumble, surprised, 'but now I'm the master.'

The stranger told the barman to fill Mr Bumble's empty glass. Then the stranger closed the door and said. 'Listen to me. I want some information from you.'

He pushed some money across the table. Mr Bumble quickly put it into his pocket.

Glossary

- **cloak:** long type of coat
- **public house:** bar

'Let's go back in time to a winter's night, nine or ten years ago. A little boy was born in the workhouse,' said the stranger. 'He was a thin pale-faced boy. He went to work for a coffin-maker, and then he ran away to London.'

'You mean Oliver! Oliver Twist!' said Mr Bumble. 'I remember him. An obstinate• young rascal•.'

'I want to know about the woman who looked after his mother. Where is she?'

'Old Sally? She died,' said Mr Bumble. 'But my wife spoke to her before she died.

The man gave Mr Bumble a piece of paper. 'Bring your wife to this address near the river tomorrow at nine. I want to speak to her,' he said.

'What name shall I ask for?' said Mr Bumble.

'Monks!' said the man, and he walked away quickly.

CHARACTERS

Who are Mr Bumble, Mrs Corney, old Sally and Monks? Go back and find out if you don't remember.

• **obstinate:** difficult

• **rascal:** dishonest person

The next evening Mr Bumble took his wife to meet Monks. It was raining hard as they reached the address near the river.

Monks stared at Mrs Bumble.

'Were you with the old woman the night she died?' Monks asked Mrs Bumble. 'What did she tell you or give you?'

'Give me twenty-five pounds in gold,' said Mrs Bumble, 'and I'll tell you everything I know.'

Monks gave the money to Mrs Bumble.

'Let's hear your story,' he said.

'A young woman had a child. The child was Oliver Twist,' said Mrs Bumble. 'The mother asked old Sally to give something to her child. But old Sally stole it. Sally told me this and then she died. In her hand I found a plain gold ring. On the inside of the ring was the name "Agnes".'

Mrs Bumble handed the ring to Monks.

Monks took the ring and threw it into the river. It fell into the water and disappeared.

'There!' said Monks, turning around. 'We can all go home. And don't say anything to anyone,' said Monks.

'Not a word,' said Mr Bumble and they left.

13 NANCY'S PLAN

16 Nancy was at Fagin's• getting some money for Sikes when there was a knock at the door.

Fagin opened the door and Monks came in. He stopped when he saw Nancy.

'It's all right. She's one of my people,' said Fagin.

Nancy ignored• them.

'Any news?' asked Fagin.

'Yes, let's talk,' said Monks.

Fagin took Monks out of the room.

Nancy silently followed the men upstairs. After fifteen minutes she returned. The two men came down the stairs and Monks left the house. Fagin went to get the money for Sikes. When he returned, Nancy was preparing to leave.

'Hurry up,' she said, 'I have to get back. Sikes doesn't want me to go out for long.'

Fagin gave Nancy the money and she left.

Later, at Sikes' house, Nancy and Sikes ate and drank. But Nancy was quiet and pale.

'You're strange, this evening,' he said. 'What's the matter•?'

'Nothing,' said Nancy. Then she waited until Sikes fell asleep. She put on her bonnet• and cloak, and hurried out of the house towards a small hotel near the park. The clock struck eleven as she went into the hotel.

Glossary

- **bonnet:** 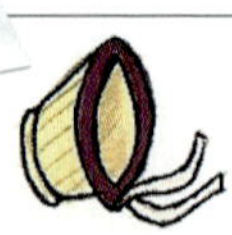
- **Fagin's:** (here) Fagin's house
- **ignored:** did not greet
- **What's the matter?:** What's the problem?

'Who are you looking for?' asked the man at the reception desk.

'A lady who is staying here,' answered Nancy. 'Miss Rose Maylie. It is very important. My name is Nancy.'

The man looked at her old clothes but he ran upstairs to ask. Then he returned a moment later.

'You can go upstairs,' he said.

'I'm Rose Maylie,' said Rose, as Nancy came to her door. 'Please tell me why you wanted to see me.'

'You know Oliver Twist. I am the girl who took little Oliver back to Fagin. Do you know a man named Monks?'

'No,' said Rose. 'I've never heard that name.'

'He knows you,' said Nancy. 'And he knows that you are staying here. I heard a conversation between Monks and Fagin. Monks is paying Fagin to find Oliver. He is paying Fagin to teach Oliver to become a thief. He will murder me if he finds out that I am telling you this.'

'Why does he want Oliver to become a thief?' asked Rose.

'I'm not sure, but I heard him say this to Fagin last night: "The only information and proof• about Oliver and his mother is at the bottom of the river. I have his money now. I want Oliver to go to prison. I want him dead. I want to kill my young brother myself!"'

'His brother!' said Rose.

OLIVER

What information do we have about Oliver now? Write a list.

• **proof:** evidence that shows something is true

'Those were his words,' Nancy continued. 'He spoke about you, too. He knows you want to find the truth about Oliver, so be careful.' Nancy looked anxious. 'It's late. I have to get home before anyone finds out that I am here.'

'Don't go back,' said Rose. 'It's too dangerous. I can find somewhere safe for you to stay.'

'I want to go back,' said Nancy, 'because there is a man that I can't leave. I don't want to be the cause of his death.'

'Where can I find you again?' asked Rose.

'Every Sunday night, between eleven and twelve,' said Nancy, 'I will walk on London Bridge.'

'Please let me help you. Take some money,' said Rose.

'No!' said Nancy. 'I feel so sorry about everything I have done. May God bless you, sweet lady, and send you happiness.'

14 NEW DISCOVERIES

17 The following morning, Oliver ran into Rose's room. He was very excited.

'I have seen Mr Brownlow,' said Oliver, 'the gentleman who was so good to me. Remember I told you about him. I saw him go into a house. Look, I have the address.' He showed Rose a piece of paper. 'Can I go there now?'

'Order the carriage,' said Rose. 'I will take you there myself.'

When they arrived, Rose left Oliver in the carriage and went into the house to speak to Mr Brownlow.

'I believe you are Mr Brownlow. Is that right?' said Rose.

'That is my name,' said the old gentleman.

'You were once very kind to a little boy.'

'Can I ask his name?' said Mr Brownlow.

'Oliver Twist,' said Rose.

Rose told Mr Brownlow Oliver's story.

'Thank God!' said Mr Brownlow. 'This makes me very happy. But where is he?'

'He is waiting in a carriage at the door,' said Rose.

And Mr Brownlow hurried out to the carriage to see Oliver. Then he called for his housekeeper, Mrs Bedwin, and Oliver was very happy to see her, too.

Mr Brownlow left Oliver and Mrs Bedwin together and led Rose into another room. There Rose told him all about her meeting with Nancy.

Mr Brownlow agreed to come back to Rose's hotel to help explain Nancy's story to Dr Losberne, who was also staying in London.

'We need a plan to catch this man Monks,' said Mr Brownlow. 'We need to speak to Nancy, and we need to keep everything a secret, especially from Oliver. He must not find out.'

'It is agreed, then,' said Dr Losberne, and the two men shook hands.

Fagin and Sikes were talking when Nancy put on her bonnet and cloak and got ready to go out.

'Where are you going at this time of night?' said Sikes.

'I need some air,' said Nancy.

'She's strange these days!' said Sikes, looking at the door.

'Let her go,' said Fagin. 'I can send one of my boys to follow her.'

Just after midnight Rose and Mr Brownlow, arrived in a carriage just a short distance from London Bridge. Nancy ran towards them.

'I can't speak to you here,' she whispered. She pointed to some steps that led to the river. There was a shadow• behind the steps.

'I hope you haven't spoken to anyone about our meeting,' said Mr Brownlow.

'No,' said Nancy.

'Good,' said Mr Brownlow. 'Now listen to me. We intend to find this man Monks and question him. If we cannot find Monks then you must give Fagin to us.'

'I will never do that!' said Nancy. 'He is bad, but I will never betray• him.'

'Then,' said Mr Brownlow, 'tell me where to find Monks and tell me what he looks like.'

Glossary

- **betray:** be disloyal to
- **shadow:** 

Nancy named the places where Mr Brownlow could find Monks and then she described him.

'He is a tall, strong man,' she said. 'When he walks he always looks over his shoulder. He has dark hair and eyes and he must be between twenty-six and twenty-eight years old, but he looks older. On his neck there is a red mark•...'

'A red mark?' said Mr Brownlow.

'Do you know him?' said Nancy.

'I think I do,' said Mr Brownlow. 'Young lady, you've helped us a lot. What can we do for you?'

'You can do nothing to help me, sir.'

'Don't go back,' said Mr Brownlow. 'We can send you somewhere safe.'

'I am chained• to my old life,' said Nancy. 'Let me go back before anyone sees me.'

'Please accept some money,' said Rose.

'No, I have not done this for money,' said Nancy. 'God bless you.'

HELP

How has Nancy helped Oliver?
Do you try to help people when you can?
Tell a friend.

Glossary

- **chained:** tied; not free (from)
- **mark:** 

15 FATAL CONSEQUENCES

18 'I've got something to tell you, Bill,' said Fagin, 'and you won't like it.'

'What's that?' said Sikes.

'One of my boys followed Nancy. On London Bridge she met a gentleman and a lady. They asked her to betray her friends. They asked her to give them information about Monks. She described him, she told them where we meet and when we go there. She told them everything,' said Fagin.

'Let me go!' cried Sikes, rushing to the door. 'Let me out,' he shouted.

'You won't be too violent, Bill?'

Sikes did not reply. He pulled open the door and ran towards home.

Nancy was lying on the bed when he went into his room.

'Someone saw you tonight,' Sikes said to Nancy. 'They heard every word you said.'

'Bill,' cried Nancy, 'stop before you hurt me! I have been true to you. I swear!'

But Sikes hit her again and again, and Nancy fell to the ground, dead.

TRUTH

Is Fagin telling the whole truth?
What did Nancy really tell Mr Brownlow?
Do YOU think it is always important to tell the truth?

16 THE MEETING WITH MONKS

Two men guarded the door while Mr Brownlow led Monks into a back room.

'What kind of treatment is this,' said Monks, 'from my father's oldest friend?'

'Yes, I was your father's oldest friend, and that is why I am treating you with kindness now,' said Mr Brownlow.

'What do you want?' said Monks.

'You have a younger half-brother called Oliver,' said Mr Brownlow.

'I do not have a brother!' cried Monks.

'You both have the same father, but not the same mother.'

'My father and mother separated,' said Monks.

'You are the first child of an unhappy marriage. Your father met another young woman called Agnes and fell in love,' said Mr Brownlow. 'They wanted to marry.'

'How nice,' said Monks.

'Your father was rich. One day he travelled to Italy but before he went he came to visit me. He told me about Agnes and gave me a portrait of her to keep. He told me that she was expecting a child. He wanted to make a new will leaving some of his money to Agnes and her child. But when your father went to Italy he became ill and died. Since your mother and father were still married when he died and the new will was not found, you and your mother automatically got all his money.'

'Your story is very long,' said Monks.

'I never saw your father again, after that visit,' Mr Brownlow continued. 'Later, I went to find Agnes. I wanted to help her, but

Glossary

- **expecting a child:** going to have a baby
- **half-brother:** (here) have the same father but different mothers
- **separated:** were not living together as husband and wife
- **treatment:** behaviour
- **will:** document that says who will receive your things when you die

her family had left a week before. No one knew where they were. Your brother Oliver came to me by chance. He was weak and neglected•. I rescued him from a life of crime.'

'What?' cried Monks.

'Oliver looked like the portrait of Agnes,' said Mr Brownlow. 'I still have the portrait hanging in my house. But somebody kidnapped Oliver before I could find out more about his past.

'You can't prove• anything against me,' said Monks.

'We shall see,' said Mr Brownlow. 'I know you are mixing with criminals. There was a will, but your mother destroyed it. It mentioned• this child. You found the child by chance. You went to the place of his birth. You found proof of his birth and who his parents were. Then you destroyed that proof. Now Nancy has been murdered and you are in part responsible.'

'It has nothing to do with me,' said Monks. 'It was a quarrel• between lovers.'

'Will you admit everything?' said Mr Brownlow. 'Give everything back to the boy and then leave.'

Monks walked up and down the room, thinking. Then he asked, 'Will this remain a secret between us?'

'It will,' said Mr Brownlow.

'Then, yes,' Monks said. 'I agree to your proposal.'

EXPLANATION

What do we now know?

Tell a friend.

- **mentioned:** talked about
- **neglected:** not loved
- **prove:** show with evidence
- **quarrel:** argument

17 THE CHASE

The situation was bad. Nancy was dead, murdered by Sikes. Fagin was in prison. So was the Dodger. Only Crackit and Charley Bates remained. And Sikes. They were all in hiding in an old warehouse in a desolate place they called Jacob's Island.

'Look!' shouted Crackit. He pointed to the window. There were policemen and a crowd gathering outside.

They could hear angry voices and the tramp of many feet.

'Murderer! Murderer!' they were shouting.

Then there was loud banging at the door.

'Help!' cried Charley Bates at the top of his voice. 'He's here! Sikes is here!'

'Damn you!' cried Sikes. He climbed out of a window and onto the roof. He had a rope and wanted to lower himself down and escape. But he slipped and fell and the rope became tight around his neck. The further he fell, the tighter the rope became. Then his body became still.

FAGIN AND HIS GANG

What happens to Fagin and his gang?
Write a list.

Glossary

- **damn you:** words used to express anger
- **desolate:** lonely
- **gathering:** coming together
- **rope:** 
- **still:** (here) without movement
- **tramp:** sound of feet
- **warehouse:** building used to keep things

18 OLIVER LEARNS MORE

21 A few days later Mr Brownlow planned a meeting between Oliver and Monks.

'This, Oliver,' said Mr Brownlow, 'is your brother, Monks.'

Oliver stared in astonishment• at Monks. Monks looked at Oliver with hate in his eyes. Mr Brownlow put his arm around Oliver.

'This, Monks, is your brother, Oliver. He is the illegitimate• son of my dear friend, your father. His mother was poor young Agnes, who died giving birth to him in the workhouse.'

'Yes, it is true,' said Monks. 'I will tell you everything that happened. My father became ill in Italy. We went to see him to say goodbye but he was too ill to recognise us, and the following day he died. He had two documents with him. One was a letter to this girl, Agnes. The other was his will.'

'Tell us about the letter,' said Mr Brownlow.

'It explains everything. Agnes was expecting my father's child. It talks of the ring he gave her, the ring with her name, Agnes, engraved• on it. And of how they wanted to get married.'

'The will,' said Mr Brownlow, 'left the money to both mothers and children in equal parts.'

'My mother burnt the will,' said Monks. 'She kept the letter and the other evidence•. We later found out that Agnes left home when my father never returned to her. No one knew where she went and everyone thought that she was dead. But my mother believed that the child was alive.'

Glossary

- **astonishment:** great surprise
- **engraved:** written on metal or stone
- **evidence:** proof
- **illegitimate:** child whose parents are not married

'And she was right,' Monks continued. 'I found him and I nearly succeeded in destroying him.'

'You paid Fagin to keep Oliver a prisoner,' said Mr Brownlow. 'Fagin even went to Mrs Maylie's house to check if Oliver was there. It wasn't Oliver's imagination when he saw Fagin and a man at the window. You were that man. What about the ring?'

'I bought it from Mrs Bumble, the mistress of the workhouse,' said Monks. 'She stole it from the nurse, old Sally, who stole it from Oliver's mother.'

Mr Brownlow suggested dividing the money from the will equally between Oliver and his older brother. He wanted to give Monks the chance to be honest. Oliver agreed. Monks took his money and moved to America.

Mr Brownlow adopted Oliver as his son. They moved, together with Mrs Bedwin, to a house close to Rose and Mrs Maylie's home in the country. Dr Losberne moved into a cottage outside the village, and the friends spent lots of time together.

And Mr and Mrs Bumble? They lost their jobs at the workhouse. With no work and no money, they had to go back to and accept charity from the same workhouse that they were once master and mistress of.

Inside the old village church, Oliver and his new family placed a marble stone with the name Agnes engraved on it. The stone is in a quiet corner. And the young woman's spirit can return to enjoy the love of her lost son: Oliver Twist.

AFTER READING

Personal Response

1 Answer these questions with a partner.

a) Did you enjoy reading the story? Why?/Why not?

b) Did you learn any new words? Tell your partner at least five new words that you learned. Which words are the easiest to remember? Which are the hardest?

c) Was there any part of the story that you didn't understand? Tell your partner.

d) What did you think of Oliver? Did you like him best or did you like another character better? Tell your partner.

e) Which character in the story would you like to be? Tell your partner.

f) Did you like the ending of the story? Can you think of a better ending?

g) Can you think of a different title for the story?

2 Do you remember what happened to the following characters at the end of the story?

Fagin

Sikes

Mr Brownlow

AFTER READING

Comprehension

1 Are the following sentences true (T) or false (F)? Tick (✓).

	T	F
a) Oliver's mother died just after she gave birth to her son.	☐	☐
b) Oliver became assistant to a doctor called Mr Sowerberry.	☐	☐
c) A boy called Jack Dawkins helped Oliver to find a place to stay in London.	☐	☐
d) Jack's real name was the Dodger.	☐	☐
e) Fagin taught Oliver how to steal.	☐	☐
f) Oliver stole Mr Brownlow's handkerchief.	☐	☐
g) Oliver looked like the young woman in the portrait.	☐	☐
h) Mr Brownlow gave Oliver a five pound note to pay for his new clothes.	☐	☐
i) Sikes needed a small boy like Oliver to help him rob a house.	☐	☐
j) Old Sally stole some gold from Oliver's mother.	☐	☐
k) Miss Rose was Mrs Maylie's sister.	☐	☐
l) Nancy listened to a conversation between Monks and Sikes.	☐	☐
m) Monks was Oliver's uncle.	☐	☐
n) Monks had dark hair and eyes and he had a red mark on his face.	☐	☐
o) Monks paid Fagin to keep Oliver a prisoner and make him become a thief.	☐	☐
p) At the end of the story, Oliver moved to America.	☐	☐

2 Match the two halves of these sentences about Oliver.

a) ☐ Oliver was a small pale thin child

b) ☐ Oliver asked for more food

c) ☐ Oliver went to work for a coffin-maker

d) ☐ Charley and the Dodger robbed Mr Brownlow

e) ☐ Fagin played the stealing game with Oliver

1 and then he ran away to London.

2 because he and the boys were hungry.

3 so that he learned to be a pickpocket.

4 but everyone believed that Oliver was the thief.

5 but he had a strong spirit.

3 When does Fagin say the following? Who is he talking to? Match his words with the right answers below.

a) ☐ Why are you watching me?

b) ☐ Clever boy. Here's a coin for you.

c) ☐ We must find our new boy Oliver before he talks to the police.

d) ☐ That boy is worth hundreds of pounds to me.

e) ☐ You won't be too violent?

1 Fagin is talking to Toby Crackit after the robbery fails.

2 Fagin is talking to Bill Sikes who is angry with Nancy.

3 Fagin is in his room, talking to Oliver.

4 Fagin is talking to Bill Sikes after the police catch Oliver.

5 Fagin is rewarding Oliver for taking a handkerchief from his pocket.

AFTER READING

Characters

1 **Match the adjectives to the characters. Then write short descriptions of each character, using the words.**

elderly powerful quiet respectable violent
pale helpful rough anxious

Nancy

quiet
pale
anxious

Mr Brownlow

respectable
helpful
elderly

Sikes

violent
powerful
rough

2 **How does Oliver feel in the following situations? Choose words from the box.**

sad horrified tired thankful angry

a) On his first night in Mr Sowerberry's shop when he had to sleep alone and is surrounded by coffins. sad

b) When Noah Claypole talked badly about his mother. angry

c) After he walked for seven days to reach London. tired

d) When the Dodger gave him food and offered him a place to stay. thankful

e) When he saw the Dodger steal Mr Brownlow's handkerchief. horrified

3 Write the names of these characters beside the sentences.

a) He works as a pickpocket and they call him the Dodger. ...Jack Dawkins...

b) He is the head of the workhouse and he gets married to Mrs Corney. ...Mr Bumble...

c) He is an ugly man with dirty red hair. He trains young children to be thieves. ...Fagin...

d) She nurses Oliver when he is sick and will not believe he is bad. ...Mrs Bedwin...

4 Who are these characters? Match their names with the descriptions.

a) [4] Old Sally
b) [2] Mr Sowerberry
c) [3] Monks
d) [1] Agnes
e) [5] Mr Brownlow

1 Oliver's mother
2 an undertaker
3 Oliver's brother
4 a nurse
5 a gentleman

5 Imagine you are a newspaper reporter. Write some questions to ask Fagin. Use these words to write your questions.

you / do / Where / live?

a) ...Where do you live?...

hide / your / box? / What / you / did / in

b) ...What did you hide in your box...

Where / those things? / get / you / did

c) ...Where did you get those things...

Oliver? / What / did / teach / game / you

d) ...What game did you teach Oliver...

6 Now work with a partner. One of you is the newspaper reporter and the other is Fagin. Ask and answer the questions.

AFTER READING

Plot and Theme

1 What happens to Oliver in the story? Put these events in the correct order.

1	2	3	4	5	6	7	8	9	10
a	j	h	b	e	f	d	g	i	**c**

a) Oliver's mother dies in the workhouse shortly after giving birth to her son.

b) Oliver arrives in London and meets Fagin, who teaches him to be a pickpocket.

c) Mr Brownlow adopts Oliver as his son and they move to a home in the country.

d) Oliver recovers from his injury in Mrs Maylie's house.

e) Everyone thinks Oliver is a thief, but Mr Brownlow asks the police to discharge him.

f) Sikes uses Oliver in a robbery, but Oliver gets shot.

g) Mr Brownlow meets with Monks, who admits that he is Oliver's half-brother.

h) Mr Sowerberry the undertaker gives Oliver a job, but Oliver runs away.

i) Helped by Mr Brownlow, Oliver meets Monks and they agree to share their father's money.

j) Oliver asks for more food and the Board orders him to leave the workhouse.

2 In the story people treat little Oliver very badly. With a partner, make a list of all the people who mistreated Oliver. What did they do to him and why did they do it?

3 **Here is a list of themes from *Oliver Twist*. Look up the words you don't know in a dictionary. Match the themes with the examples below.**

a) ☐ Dishonesty b) ☐ Loyalty c) ☐ Identity
d) ☐ Greed e) ☐ Poverty

1 The boys in the workhouse get the charity of the town, but they never have enough to eat.
2 Fagin is bad, but Nancy will not betray him.
3 Mr Bumble sells information about Oliver to Mr Brownlow and to Monks. Monks wants Oliver's money.
4 Mrs Bumble stole a ring from old Sally, who stole it from Oliver's mother.
5 Oliver doesn't know the name of his mother or his father.

K 4 **Read part of this letter from Rose to Mrs Maylie. Choose the best word (a, b or c) for each space.**

Last night a young woman visited me at my (1)........... . Her name was Nancy. She was the girl who took little Oliver back to (2)........... . She talked about a man called Monks. Monks is paying Fagin to teach Oliver to become a (3)........... . Monks had information about Oliver and his mother, but now that information is at the bottom of the (4)........... . Monks has Oliver's money now. He wants Oliver to go to (5)........... .

1	a) shop	b) hotel	c) cottage
2	a) Mr Bumble	b) Mr Sowerberry	c) Fagin
3	a) doctor	b) thief	c) teacher
4	a) river	b) cooking pot	c) cellar
5	a) school	b) church	c) prison

AFTER READING

Language

1 Read these sentences and choose the present perfect or the past simple. Circle the correct answer.

a) The wind *has blown/blew* and it *has rained/rained* hard when Oliver and Sikes *started/have started* their journey.

b) 'Oliver is nine years old now,' said Mr Bumble. 'He's too old to stay at the orphanage so we *decided/have decided* to move him to the workhouse. I *have come/came* here myself to collect him and take him there.

c) 'Here,' said Mr Brownlow, 'this is a five pound note. Give the bookshop owner the books and say you *have come/came* to pay the money I owe him.' Oliver *has gone out/went out* and Mr Brownlow *has waited/waited* for him to return.

2 Use the following reflexive pronouns to complete these sentences.

myself	yourself	himself
herself	ourselves	themselves

a) When you are poor and have no family, you have to learn to take care of ...yourself... .

b) The boys at the workhouse had no money and could not feed ...themselves...

c) 'I want Oliver dead,' said Monks. 'I want to kill my young brother ...myself...!'

d) Sikes had a rope and wanted to lower ...himself... down from the roof and escape.

e) When Oliver wanted to go to Mr Brownlow's house, Rose ordered the carriage and took him there ...herself...

f) The police aren't doing enough to fight crime in our cities so we will have to catch the criminals ...ourselves... .

3 Match the answers to the questions.

a) ☐ When is Monks meeting Mr and Mrs Bumble?
b) ☐ What is Sikes planning to do later tonight?
c) ☐ What are they serving for dinner in the workhouse next Sunday?
d) ☐ When is Oliver leaving for London?
e) ☐ Who is Nancy visiting after Sikes goes to sleep?

1 Thin soup with half a piece of bread.
2 To rob a house.
3 She's visiting Rose at her hotel.
4 They're meeting tomorrow night.
5 Early tomorrow morning.

4 Agree with the following remarks. Use *Neither do I* or *So do I.*

a) I don't like Sikes. ....
b) I like Rose. ....
c) I don't want Fagin to be executed. ....
d) I want Monks to make friends with Oliver. ....
e) I don't want Oliver to be a criminal. ....

5 Fill the blanks with the correct form of the verbs.

a) Nancy and Sikes .... Oliver and took him back to Fagin. (kidnap)
b) Oliver .... but Sikes had a powerful grip. (struggle)
c) Nancy .... Sikes because she loved him. (not/betray)
d) Sikes planned to .... a house, but the robbery failed. (rob)
e) Oliver had no parents so Mr Brownlow .... him. (adopt)

AFTER READING

Exit Test

1 Listen and choose the correct picture.

a) 1

2

b) 1

2

c) 1

2

d) 1

2

K 2 **Read the sentences about the story and choose the best word (1, 2 or 3) for each space.**

a) Oliver is an .... because he has no father and his mother died after she gave birth to him.

1 apprentice 2 criminal 3 orphan

b) Oliver runs away to London where he meets a young .... called the Dodger.

1 pickpocket 2 undertaker 3 housekeeper

c) The police officer accuses Oliver of robbing Mr Brownlow, but discharges him because he is ....

1 afraid 2 innocent 3 violent

d) Oliver has to rob a house with Sikes, but the robbery fails and Oliver is ....

1 killed 2 kidnapped 3 wounded

e) Monks is Oliver's .... because he has the same father but not the same mother.

1 uncle 2 half-brother 3 younger brother

3 **With a partner, look at the picture on page 61. Ask and answer questions about it.**

Who is the man on the roof?

It's Bill Sikes.

What is he doing?

He's trying to escape.

AFTER READING
Project

CREATE A CHARLES DICKENS NEWSPAPER

Charles Dickens worked as a journalist and wrote for newspapers and magazines. His stories appeared a few chapters at a time in some of these publications. In 1846 he founded a newspaper called The Daily News, in this project you will design, write and edit your own Charles Dickens-style newspaper.

a) Do some background research first. Collect some newspapers and magazines. Try to find some that are in English as well as in your own language. Look through them and make a list of the articles they contain.
Did you find any of these?
- Crime reports
- Opinion articles
- Advertisements
- Fashion pages
- Letters to the editor

b) Now make a list of events from *Oliver Twist* that you can write about for your newspaper. Here are some examples:
- A crime report about a gang of boys who are picking the pockets of rich gentlemen.
- A description of the latest fashions for men and women.
- An article criticising the workhouses.
- A letter to the editor saying that the police are not doing enough to fight crime.

c) Work with your team of reporters to write short articles about some of the above.

WEB d) Illustrate your newspaper project with images from the internet.

e) Post your newspaper around the classroom for everyone to read.